A First Look at Art

Places

Ruth Thomson

Chrysalis Children's Books

First published in the UK in 2003 by
Chrysalis Children's Books
An imprint of Chrysalis Books Group Plc,
The Chrysalis Building, Bramley Road
London W10 6SP

ISBN 1 84138 705 3

British Library Cataloguing in Publication Data for this
book is available from the British Library.

Editorial manager: Joyce Bentley
Editor: Susie Brooks
Designers: Rachel Hamdi, Holly Mann
Picture researchers: ilumi, Aline Morley
Illustrator: Linda Francis
Photographer: Steve Shott
Consultant: Erika Langmuir, formerly Head
of Education, The National Gallery, London

The author and publishers would like to thank
the following people for their contributions to this book:
Joanne Acty and children from Artworks, Oxford; Jan
Geddes, Richard Hutchinson, Michael Mitchell, Chris
Miles and children from Laycock Primary School,
Islington, London; Elizabeth Emerson.

Printed in China

Picture acknowledgements
Front cover: AKG London/© DACS
2003. **4**: Bridgeman Art Library; **5**:
Bridgeman Art Library/©Estate of
Stanley Spencer 2003. All Rights
Reserved, DACS; **6/7**: Bridgeman
Art Library/©Estate of Grant
Wood/VAGA, New York/DACS,
London 2003; **10/11**: Bridgeman Art
Library/©ADAGP, Paris and DACS,
London 2003; **14/15**: National Gallery
of Art, Washington, 1982.35.1/© ARS,
NY and DACS, London 2003; **18**:
AKG London/©Estate of Stuart
Davis/VAGA, New York/DACS, London
2003; **19**: Alfred Stieglitz Collection,
Fisk University Galleries/©ARS, NY
and DACS, London 2003; **22**: National
Gallery of Art, Washington, 1970.17.45; **23**: Bridgeman
Art Library; **26/27**: Bridgeman Art Library/© DACS 2003

Contents

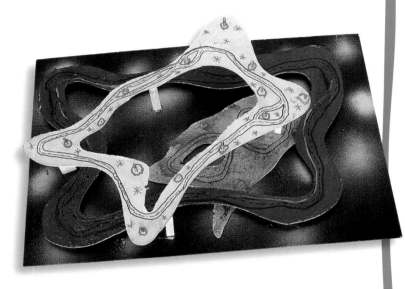

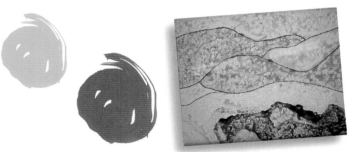

PICTURE A PLACE

Places have always inspired artists. Lush countryside, sunny coasts and busy cities are just a few examples. In this book you'll see how some artists have depicted real places, while others have worked from their imagination. You'll find out what influenced the artists and learn about their techniques. We've included questions to help you look at the works of art in detail. There are also ideas for creating your own pictures and sculptures of places both real and imaginary.

⦿ You'll find answers to the questions and information about the artists on pages 30 and 31.

Arty tips

✧ Look out for Arty tips boxes that suggest handy techniques and materials to use in your own work.

Picture hunt

✧ Picture hunt boxes suggest other artists and artworks that you might like to look at.

The Canal Bridge
L. S. Lowry
1949
(71 x 91.2cm)

Cookham from Cookham Dean
Stanley Spencer
1938 (66 x 117cm)

Choosing the view

When artists paint places, they make lots of choices that help them to create the right atmosphere. One thing they need to pick is a viewpoint. In the picture on the left we look down a long city street. Lowry has painted it from high up – perhaps from the window of a building. Spencer's wide country valley, above, is viewed from a gentle grassy slope.

Finding a focus

Artists also have to decide what details to include and emphasise in their scenes. Lowry's painting focuses on the road, with people trudging along it. Tall factory chimneys crowd the skyline and frame the picture on either side. Spencer's painting focuses on the open countryside. Lines of hedges and trees lead your eye in a zigzag to the faraway hills.

Colour and mood

Artists can create certain moods by the way they use colour. Greys and black dominate Lowry's picture, suggesting the harshness of life in a smoky city. Calm greens and gold in Spencer's picture create a more peaceful atmosphere. When you look at other pictures of places, think about the way that the artists felt about them. Would you feel the same?

A COUNTRY SCENE

Paintings of the open countryside are called landscapes. They are often shaped like this one, where the width of the canvas is greater than its height.

Open spaces

Artists can create landscapes that seem to stretch for miles. Follow the route of the horse and rider. See how the artist leads your eye along the winding road.

◉ What will the horse and rider pass on their countryside journey?

Into the distance

Notice how the road narrows in the distance. Eventually, it disappears at a point on the far horizon where the land meets the sky. This is known by artists as the vanishing point.

Stone City Grant Wood
1930 (77 x 101.5cm)

Artist's tricks

The artist has used several other tricks to make things appear nearby or further away.

See how objects that are bigger, bolder and more detailed seem the closest to you. Things that are fainter, smaller and higher up in the painting appear to be further away.

Notice how things overlap. The line of dark trees on the left overlaps the hills. This makes the trees appear to be in front of the hills and therefore much closer.

◉ Which wind turbine seems the furthest away?
◉ Which building seems the nearest?
◉ Which of the hills is most distant?
◉ Which part of the painting seems closest to you?

LOOKING AT LANDSCAPES

From the hilltops

Stand on a hilltop with a wide open view and draw what you can see.

◉ Concentrate on the outlines of buildings, trees and shrubs that are both near and far away.

Molly, aged 8

Kayla, aged 8

Make a viewfinder

Artists often use a frame called a viewfinder to choose a good view. They hold it at arm's length and look through it to decide what to paint.

◉ Make a viewfinder of your own by cutting a rectangular frame from a piece of stiff card.

Choose a view

◉ Use your viewfinder to select and draw a view. Add different textures for the ground, trees and buildings.

Philly, aged 7

Picture hunt

✧ Compare works by some famous artists, such as John Constable, Claude Monet, Vincent Van Gogh, Paul Cézanne and Camille Pissarro. Notice how they create a feeling of space, distance and atmosphere in their landscape paintings.

A textured landscape

Make a collage picture of a real or imaginary landscape.

◉ Use materials that suit the place, such as real sand and shells for a beach, dried grass, flowers or straw for fields, stones for a path or rocky shore, and twigs and leaves for trees.

Ned, aged 7

Helen, aged 9

◉ Alternatively, use scraps of fabric with different textures and patterns to represent hills, water, sky and earth.

Model scenery

Create a 3-D model of a landscape.

◉ Take a piece of hardboard or stiff card for the base, and paint it.

◉ Glue lumps of scrumpled paper on to the base to make hills. Leave gaps between them for valleys.

◉ Cover the surface with layers of papier maché (see below) to create a smooth, rolling landscape.

◉ Use card tubes for tree trunks and stick on leaves and flowers cut from coloured paper or fabric.

Xara, aged 9

Arty tips

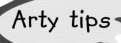

✿ Use PVA glue for making collages.

✿ Mix PVA glue with water to make papier mâché (use equal amounts of both). Dip torn paper strips into the runny glue and layer them at angles across one another for strength.

A PERSONAL PLACE

Sometimes artists are inspired by one particular place. Dufy, who painted this scene, was fascinated by the clear light and intense blue sea of Nice, on the south coast of France.

Admire the view

Here, Dufy invites us to come into his bright, sun-drenched room. Through the open windows we can see a view of the sunny coastline that intrigued the artist so much.

◉ How does Dufy separate the room from the view beyond?

◉ What do you think the marks leading out from the right-hand window might indicate?

◉ How does Dufy show reflections and shadows?

Inside

The contrasting yellows and blues and the rich red carpet make Dufy's room glow with warmth. The white flowers bring a touch of the natural world indoors.

◉ How does Dufy show what is in the rest of the room, behind our viewpoint?

Outside

The lines of the French windows frame a fresh, airy view of the sea, sky and town outside.

Notice how Dufy has painted things in the far distance very sketchily. The trees are black blobs, the bobbing yachts are upturned V-shapes and the buildings are just a series of lines and blocks of colour.

Interior with Open Windows
Raoul Dufy
1928 (66 x 82cm)

YOUR ROOM AND VIEW

Through the window

Draw or paint the view you can see from a window at home or at school.

◉ Cut a sheet of clear acetate the same size as your picture. Lay it on top.

◉ Make a window frame to fit over the acetate, using card or thin wooden strips. Glue the frame in place.

Samantha, aged 11

Hermione, aged 10

Shelley, aged 11

Picture hunt

✧ Compare Dufy's **Interior with Open Windows** with **Interior at Nice** and **Landscape viewed from a Window** by Henri Matisse, or **The Breakfast Room** by Pierre Bonnard. Notice how they contrast the inside of a room with the scene outside.

◉ To suggest the room inside, stick the picture on to some wallpaper or on to a sheet of paper you have decorated.

Frame the view

Make a frame for one of your landscape pictures, so that you can hang it on a wall in your room.

◉ Lay your picture in the centre of a sheet of card. Draw around the edges of your picture.

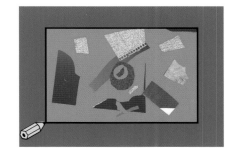

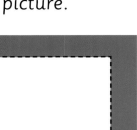

◉ Cut along the lines you have drawn.

◉ Paint and decorate your card frame.

Khari, aged 11

◉ Tape your picture to the back of the frame. Attach a piece of string so you can hang it up.

Arty tip

✫ If you want to make a textured frame with raised patterns, glue some rolled or folded paper, some pasta, string or shells on to the frame. Leave it to dry, then paint it or cover it with silver foil.

A shoebox room

Use a shoebox to create a room with a painted view or painted window.

◉ Cut one or more windows and a doorway in the box.

◉ Paint the inside of the box to look like the walls, floor and ceiling of a room.

Lucy, aged 11

◉ Paint an outside view on a sheet of paper, to fit across the window holes.

◉ Alternatively, paint a colourful pattern on some tracing paper, so it looks like stained glass.

◉ Tape the paper in place.

Jarama II
Frank
Stella
1982
(319.9 x
253.9 x
62.8cm)

Artists don't always want to
show what a place *looks* like.
Sometimes they prefer to
capture the *atmosphere* of
a place, by suggesting what
it feels or sounds like.

A roaring racetrack

In this work, Frank Stella shows
the thrill he gets from watching
roaring, zooming racing cars
speed around a track. Its title,
Jarama II, is named after
a racing circuit in Spain.

A tangle of metal

Separate, curving, painted metal
tracks criss-cross one another
here. They suggest the way
racing cars zig-zag back and
forth when they overtake each
other at top speed. The tangle
of metal could also represent
the dangers of car racing.

See how the pieces jut out
from the wall at different levels.
This kind of artwork is called
a relief – it's a cross between
a painting and a sculpture.

Imagine yourself at a racetrack
while you look at this piece.

- Follow the different coloured
tracks with your finger. How
many tracks can you find?
- Where you do think the
race might begin or end?
- Which marks resemble the
trail of car exhausts?
- How does Stella conjure up
the heat and noise of powerful
car engines?
- What do the dotted green
lines remind you of?

CAPTURE THE FEELING

Zoom, zooooom!

Create your own roaring racetrack.

◉ Draw several racetrack circuits on stiff card. Cut them out.

◉ Paint them with marks that suggest the speed and noise of racing cars.

◉ Paint a large sheet of cardboard or hardboard for the background.

◉ Glue the racing circuits at different levels on to the background. Use wood offcuts or pieces of thick card or dowel to separate the tracks.

Krystal, aged 10

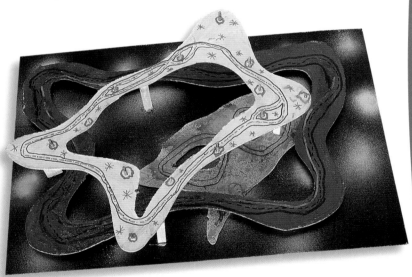

A thrilling ride

Make a collage of a spine-tingling ride, such as a big wheel or a rollercoaster.

◉ Paint a sky on some card or paper.

◉ Use string, fabric scraps and other found materials to construct your ride.

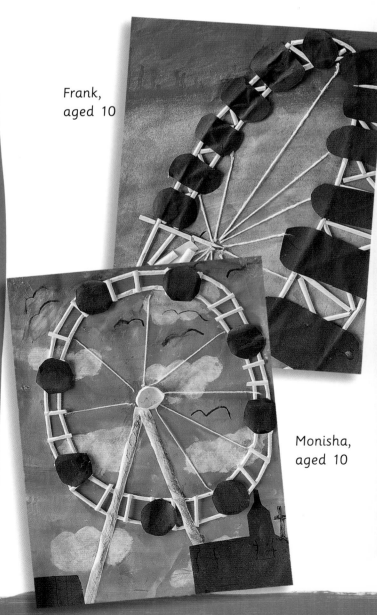

Frank, aged 10

Monisha, aged 10

Picture hunt

✧ See how other artists have suggested the energy and excitement of a particular place or event, such as **Battle of the Lights, Coney Island** by Joseph Stella; **Eiffel Tower** by Robert Delauney and **Montorgueil Street in Paris, Celebration of June 30, 1878** by Claude Monet.

Use all your senses

Think about what you can see, hear and feel in a particular place, such as at home, in a park, by the sea, at a football match or at a show.

◉ Write down your sensations.
◉ Make a collage picture that expresses those sensations.

Home
Tomilayo and Zeynep

Enjoy the cosy atmosphere.
Feel the freedom.
Experience the fun.
Imagine the safety.
Feel the warmth.
Touch the comfort.

The concert
Musharrifaq, Abdul and Chase

See the glittering lights shining in your eyes.
Feel the calmness building to excitement.
See the shadows of the singers
dancing on stage.
Feel the vibrations of the bass.
Hear the children screaming with excitement.
Feel your heart beating with happiness.
See the entrance door opening and closing.
See the people jumping up and down.
Feel the songs travel through your body.

Arty tip

✪ Use different materials to represent each feeling. In these two pictures the springs show excitement, the tinsel represents lights, the red fluffy material suggests warmth and the curled paper expresses fun. What else could you use?

BRIGHT CITY LIGHTS

New York under Gaslight *Stuart Davis 1941 (81.3 x 114.3cm)*

These two pictures show contrasting views of New York, a noisy, energetic city that is busy 24 hours a day.

Signs of life

For the painting above, Davis was inspired by the everyday sights he saw across the street from a shop. Notice the shop canopy stretching across the top of the scene with its handle hanging down.

Davis used a variety of shapes, patterns and signs in clashing, sizzling colours to suggest the buzzing activity of city life.

◉ Is it day or night in Davis's picture? What two clues show you this?

◉ Can you find these shapes or patterns somewhere in the picture?

- zig-zags
- rectangles
- criss-cross grids
- stripes
- stars
- brick patterns

Twinkling tower

Here, O'Keeffe has concentrated on a single skyscraper. It had only recently been built when she painted it. The building towers above the rest of the city, with light from its pinnacle and windows gleaming brightly in the dark night sky.

O'Keeffe suggests busy city life by including beaming searchlights, wafting smoke and the glow of street lamps on the pavement.

◉ How has O'Keeffe suggested the presence of lots of people in her painting?

◉ What colours has O'Keeffe used for the artificial city lights?

◉ How has O'Keeffe emphasised the great height of the skyscraper?

◉ Which of the two pictures do you think is better at capturing the feeling of a big city? Why?

Radiator Building – Night, New York Georgia O'Keeffe
1927 (121.9 x 76.2cm)

NIGHT SIGHTS

The city skyline

◉ Cut out shapes of skyscrapers and other buildings from black or grey paper.
◉ Glue them on to a sheet of paper that you've painted dark blue.
◉ Draw in lots of brightly lit windows using a soft white crayon.

Kerise, aged 11

Khalida, aged 11

Picture hunt

✦ Look at these pictures by other artists who painted city scenes at night: **The Brooklyn Bridge** by Joseph Stella; **The Café Terrace at Arles at Night** by Vincent van Gogh; **The Boulevard Montmartre at Night** by Camille Pissarro; **Nighthawks** by Edward Hopper.

City silhouettes

◉ Cut out some tall buildings from black paper. Cut holes for their windows.
◉ Cut trees, people and animals from black paper as well.
◉ Arrange the pieces on a large sheet of tracing paper to create a busy city scene. Glue them in place.
◉ Shine a light on the picture from behind and admire the effect! A coloured light bulb works well.

Joel, aged 8

Shining lights

Use intense contrasts between light and dark to paint an exciting night scene that's glowing with bright electric lights.

◉ Paint the night sky either pitch black or very dark blue.

◉ Use strong, bright colours to make the buildings stand out.

◉ Use yellow or white paint for the beams or pinpricks of light.

◉ Outline any figures, or highlight parts of their faces in white.

Freya, aged 11

Ella, aged 11

Arty tip

✰ Decide what direction the light is coming from in your scene. If it's from the left, highlight the left side of things, and so on.

21

The Artist's Garden at Vétheuil Claude Monet
1880 (151.4 x 121cm)

Snow at Louveciennes
Alfred Sisley
1878 (61 x 50.5cm)

Monet and Sisley were interested in the changing effects of natural light. They tried to capture on canvas an exact moment in time. They avoided using sharp outlines or precise details. Instead, they painted with dabs and dashes of colour.

Heat and chill

In the painting on the left, Monet has created a sense of hazy heat. He used bright, contrasting colours that sizzle when placed side by side.

Sisley used a narrow range of drab colours to suggest the chilly feel of a grey winter's day.

◉ Which colours make one picture feel warm and the other feel cold?

◉ What time of day is it in Monet's garden? How can you tell?

◉ Why did the artists include people? Hide them with your finger. What difference does it make without them?

FEEL THE HEAT

Warm and cool colours

Red, orange and yellow make us think of the sun, leaping flames and glowing lights. These are known as warm colours. They can create feelings of energy and excitement in pictures.

Blue, green and grey are known as cool colours because they remind us of ice, water, damp clouds and chilly fog. Cool colours can create an atmosphere of calm, quiet or gloom.

Picture hunt

✧ Look at summery pictures of haystacks, harvests and wheatfields by Vincent Van Gogh. Notice the strong colours he uses.

✧ Look at other snowy scenes, such as **Hunters in the Snow** by Pieter Brueghel or **The Magpie** by Claude Monet, and wintery pictures by Hendrick Avercamp of people enjoying themselves on the ice.

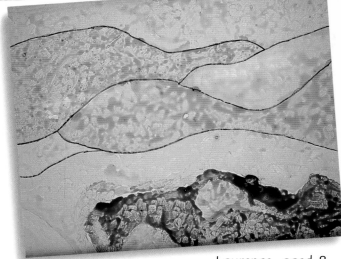

Laurence, aged 8

Sun-drenched

◉ Draw a sunny landscape on clear perspex, using a permanent marker.
◉ Dab water-based glass paint on the perspex to create a textured surface.
◉ Put the picture in a place where light can shine through it and make it glow and shimmer.

Matthew, aged 8

Ice-cold

◉ Use a variety of cool colours to paint a picture that will make people shiver when they look at it.

Seasonal collages

Make a collage that conjures up the feeling of a particular season.

◉ For the background, choose a colour that is typical of the season you have chosen.

Spring

Kristina, aged 8

Summer

Carolyn, aged 12

◉ Cut out paper shapes that help show what the season is like. For example, long, spiky shapes might suggest winter icicles; petal shapes could suggest spring flowers.

Autumn

Camilla, aged 12

Winter

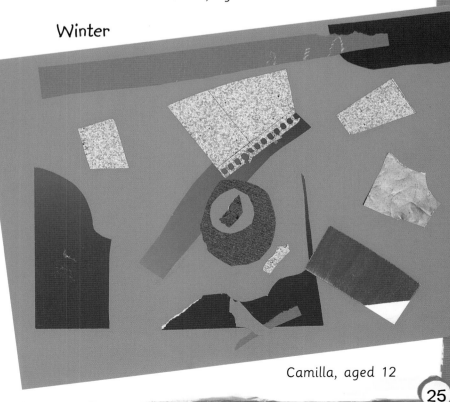

Camilla, aged 12

Arty tips

✶ Tear paper instead of cutting it, if you want a rough effect.

✶ Use shiny, patterned and textured papers or fabrics, as well as plain colours.

✶ Put some of the shapes on top of one another to create layers.

AN IMAGINARY PLACE

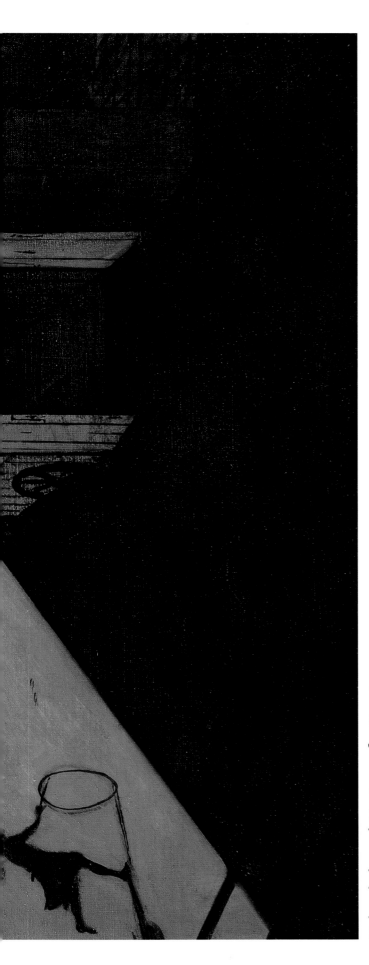

Melancholy and Mystery of a Street
Giorgio de Chirico 1914 (88 x 72cm)

Some artists paint the places of their daydreams. Giorgio de Chirico painted pictures of still, strange, silent cities. This one is full of puzzling features that invite us to ask questions. Who is the girl? Why is she in this place? Where is she going? Why is there an open railway wagon here? Who is around the corner?

◉ Ask yourself questions and make up your own story about this picture.

A curious city

De Chirico included buildings from real places in his pictures – particularly places in Italy where he lived. In the centre of many Italian cities is an open square, often with the statue of a hero in it. Around the square are covered walkways called arcades, where people can stroll out of the sun.

Here, De Chirico hints at the view of a square, but he doesn't show it in a realistic way. The arcades and shadows are at odd angles and we can see only the shadow of a heroic statue.

◉ What catches your eye first and draws you into the picture?

◉ Choose three words to describe the mood of the painting. How does it make you feel?

◉ What clue tells you that it must be a windy day?

◉ Where is the light coming from?

IN YOUR DREAMS

Strange roads

Create a strange, dreamy street scene of your own.

Paris, aged 11

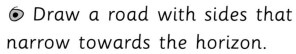

◉ Draw a road with sides that narrow towards the horizon.

◉ Draw buildings on either side, with walls that appear to become smaller as they get further away.

◉ Add some people and paint the scene in dramatic, clashing colours.

Noah, aged 11

Rio, aged 11

◉ Alternatively, draw two roads going in different directions from the corner where they meet.

◉ Draw a building on the corner, with its two sides sloping towards the horizon.

◉ Paint something strange happening on your weird and wonderful street.

Conisha, aged 11

Land of make-believe

Paint a picture of an imaginary place. Think of answers to some of these questions before you start painting.

◉ What is the landscape like? Is it flat or hilly, lush or rocky? Is it surrounded by sea? Are there waterfalls, volcanoes, craters or canyons?

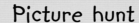

Picture hunt

✬ Artists such as René Magritte, Leonora Carrington, Max Ernst, Yves Tanguy and Kay Sage all created dream-like pictures. Compare some of their images, where real and imaginary things and people are mixed together in bizarre ways.

Meredith, aged 8

◉ What grows in this place?
◉ What is the weather like?
◉ Who lives here? How did they get here? What do they look like? What do they live in? What is their lifestyle like?
◉ Think of a good name for your imaginary place. You could even create a map showing where the place is.

Arty tip

✬ To make your pictures more dream-like, paint people and things in unexpected colours. Trees might have orange leaves, water might be pink and people might have green hair or purple skin.

Freya, aged 8

29

ARTISTS AND ANSWERS

PICTURE A PLACE (pages 4/5)

About L. S. LOWRY

Lowry (1887-1976) lived all his life near Manchester, a large industrial city in northern England. Many of his pictures are busy city scenes showing ordinary working people going about their everyday lives.

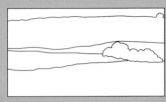

About STANLEY SPENCER

Spencer (1891-1959) was also an English artist. He is perhaps best-known for his imaginative pictures of bible stories, set in the Thameside village of Cookham where he spent his childhood. He also painted many landscapes and portraits of himself and his family. During World War II, he was an official war artist.

A COUNTRY SCENE (pages 6/7)

Answers for pages 6 and 7

• The horse and rider will cross the bridge, passing a farm and wind turbine, then they'll go past a factory, a water tower, another farm, fields and an orchard.

• The small turbine near the horizon seems the furthest.
• The red L-shaped barn seems the nearest building.
• The hill that is highest in the picture and nearest to the horizon line seems the most distant.
• The field at the bottom of the picture seems nearest.

About GRANT WOOD

Wood (1891-1942) grew up on a small farm in Iowa, mid-west America. His country childhood influenced a lot of his work, such as scenes of rolling farmland, views of village life and humorous portraits of local people. Wood studied at art schools in America and travelled to Europe to visit galleries. His precise, crisp style was inspired by 15th-century Flemish artists, who painted in a very clear and detailed way.

A PERSONAL PLACE (pages 10/11)

Answers for page 10

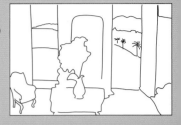

• Dufy separates the room from outside with the red carpet, the window frames and balcony rails.
• The marks might indicate steps down to the beach.
• He shows reflections by adding dashes of white paint. He creates shadows by using darker colours.
• The rest of the room is shown in the mirror.

About RAOUL DUFY

Dufy (1877-1953) grew up in the French port of Le Havre then moved to Paris. There, he was influenced by the paintings of Henri Matisse, who used unusually strong colours. Dufy developed his own style, using bright colours with sketchy outlines. He painted light-hearted, sunny scenes of the seaside town of Nice, as well as regattas (boat races) and horse races. He also illustrated books and designed fabrics and ceramics.

A PLACE OF EXCITEMENT (pages 14/15)

Answers for page 14

• There are eight different tracks.
• The race doesn't seem to have a definite start or finish.
• The white scribbly marks might suggest the trail of car exhausts.
• 'Hot' colours (red, orange and yellow) and jagged marks suggest the heat and noise of the cars.
• The green dotted lines could remind you of road markings, cars moving along the track or speed marks.

About FRANK STELLA

Stella (b. 1936) is an American abstract painter. His early paintings were large canvases of black parallel lines with patterned bands of colour. Later, he used shaped canvases, painted with colourful or metallic stripes that follow the shape of the canvas. He moved on to making painted, cut metal wall-objects (reliefs), and then to making huge cut-metal structures.

BRIGHT CITY LIGHTS (pages 18/19)
Answers for page 18

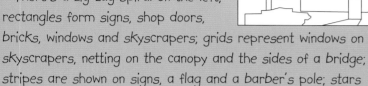

- The light in the shop and the moon in the sky show that it is night.
- There's a zig-zag spiral on the left; rectangles form signs, shop doors, bricks, windows and skyscrapers; grids represent windows on skyscrapers, netting on the canopy and the sides of a bridge; stripes are shown on signs, a flag and a barber's pole; stars are on the triangular roof; bricks are on buildings and rubble.

About Stuart Davis

Davis (1894-1964) was an American painter. His work was strongly influenced by modern city sights, particularly signs and adverts. He was also inspired by jazz music. He used mainly strong colours and flat-looking shapes, and often put words in his paintings.

Answers for page 19

- The illuminated windows suggest the presence of lots of people.
- O'Keeffe has used white, yellow, orange, grey and red for the artificial city lights.
- O'Keeffe has painted the skyscraper from below to emphasise its height.

About Georgia O'Keeffe

O'Keeffe (1887-1986) is perhaps America's most famous woman painter. She was born on a farm in Wisconsin, and decided early in life to become an artist. She painted American places, such as Lake George, New York and New Mexico. She is also known for her close-up paintings of flowers, bones, stones and fruit.

SUNSHINE AND SNOW
(pages 22/23) Answers for page 23

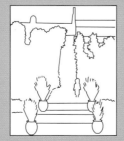

- Red, yellow and orange make Monet's picture feel warm. Grey, blue and white make Sisley's picture feel cold.
- It is probably late afternoon in Monet's garden, because you can see long shadows.

- The artists included people to lead your eye along the paths into their pictures, as well as to give a sense of scale. Without the people, it would be difficult to tell how big or small the other objects in the pictures might be.

About CLAUDE MONET

Monet (1840-1926) grew up on the north coast of France. A local artist encouraged him to paint out in the open air, instead of indoors as most painters did. Monet then moved to Paris and befriended other artists, such as Alfred Sisley, Pierre Auguste Renoir and Camille Pissarro. He persuaded them to paint outdoors as well. They developed a style known as Impressionism, named after one of Monet's paintings.

About ALFRED SISLEY

Sisley (1839-1890), a British artist, was born in Paris, France. He became friends with Monet and Renoir and painted with them in the countryside. He was among the group of artists that showed their work in the first Impressionist exhibition in 1874. Sisley spent his lifetime painting landscapes, gardens and city scenes, but he had little success in selling his work.

AN IMAGINARY PLACE
(pages 26/27) Answers for page 27

- The girl, or perhaps the long white building, might have caught your eye first.
- You might choose the following words to describe the mood of de Chirico's picture: strange, mysterious, puzzling, unsettling, quiet, silent, spooky, chilly, scary, eerie, menacing, alarming, odd, hushed. What other words did you think of?
- The flying flag shows that it must be a windy day.
- The light appears to come from both left and right.

About GIORGIO DE CHIRICO

De Chirico (1888-1978) was Italian, but he grew up partly in Greece. He trained as an engineer before becoming a painter. He is best known for his early paintings of mysterious dream-like cityscapes, drawn from real places. In his later life he worked in a more realistic style, painting mostly landscapes, Roman villas and horses.

GLOSSARY

atmosphere The feeling or mood of a place.

canvas A stiff cloth that artists use to paint on.

collage A picture made by sticking bits of paper, fabric, or other objects, on to a background.

horizon The line where the land meets the sky.

Impressionism An art movement in which artists painted out in the open air and focused on the effects of light.

interior An indoor scene.

landscape A countryside scene.

relief A raised artwork that is based on a flat surface – a cross between a painting and a sculpture.

texture How something feels to the touch, for example rough or smooth.

vanishing point A point on the horizon where parallel lines (eg the sides of a road) appear to meet.

viewfinder A frame used by an artist to pick a view.

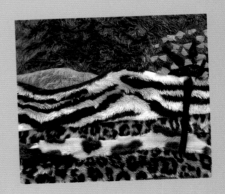